Rookie Read-About™ Science

W9-BEG-352

Tasting Things

By Allan Fowler

Images supplied by VALAN Photos

Consultants:
Robert L. Hillerich, Ph.D., Bowling Green
State University, Bowling Green, Ohio

Mary Nalbandian, Director of Science,
Chicago Public Schools, Chicago, Illinois

Fay Robinson, Child Development Specialist

CHILDRENS PRESS®
CHICAGO

Series Cover and interior design by Sara Shelton

Library of Congress Cataloging-in-Publication Data

Fowler, Allan.
    Tasting things / by Allan Fowler.
        p.   cm.—(Rookie read-about science)
    Summary: A simple introduction to the sense of taste.
    ISBN 0-516-04911-9
    1. Taste—Juvenile literature. [1. Taste. 2. Senses and
sensation.] I. Title. II. Series.
QP456.F69 1991
612.8'7—dc20   90-21647
                                                                    CIP
                                                                    AC

Someone's baking cookies!

You can tell by the
wonderful smell. And the
cookies look as good as
they smell. Then you
hear, "They're ready to
eat." You pick one up and
it feels warm and crumbly.

You have just used four
of your senses—smell,
sight, hearing, and touch.

Now it's time to put the cookie in your mouth, and to enjoy it by using your fifth sense, your sense of taste.

Eating is fun. There are
so many kinds of foods
to taste.

Each food has a flavor of its own.

What does it taste like?
Is it

sweet,

sour,

salty,

17

or many tastes at once?

How do you taste all these flavors?

Try this.

Look in the mirror and stick out your tongue. Go ahead! The person in the mirror won't mind.

See all those tiny bumps that cover your tongue? Those bumps are called taste buds. They help you taste food.

A food's smell is also part of its taste. When your nose is stuffed, you can't smell what you're eating.

Try this.

Pinch your nose with your fingers. Take a bite of an apple. Now let go of your nose and take another bite. Can you taste the difference?

Taste can be a funny thing. You might think a certain food tastes great,

while your friend won't
like it at all.

Sometime, you may be offered food you have never eaten before.

Will you like it?

You can't tell just by looking at it.

So taste it!

What is your favorite food?

What does it taste like?

Words You Know

sense of taste

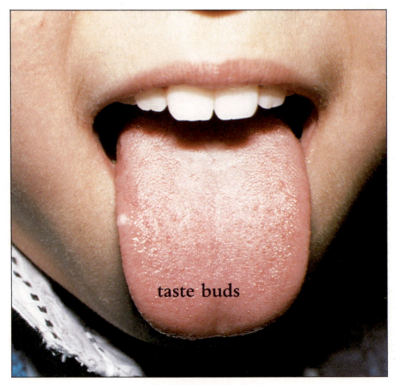

taste buds

tongue

a salty food

a sweet food

a sour food

Index

About the Author

Allan Fowler is a free-lance writer with a background in advertising. Born in New York, he lives in Chicago now and enjoys traveling.

Photo Credits

Valan—© Wouterloot—Gregoire, Cover, 9, 14; © V. Wilkinson, 3, 5, 6, 15, 16, 17, 18, 19, 21, 23, 30, 31, (top left & bottom); © V. Momatiuk/J. Eastcott, 8; © Richard Nowit, 10; © Kennon Cooke, 11, 25, 27, 28; © Prof. R. C. Simpson, 13; © Phil Norton, 31 (top right)
COVER: Crazy face salad